Children
of the
CIVIL RIGHTS ERA

Children
of the
CIVIL RIGHTS ERA

Catherine A. Welch

Carolrhoda Books, Inc./Minneapolis

To John and Michael

Front cover: Black students arrive at Clinton High School in Tennessee in 1956. Before a court ruling forced the school to accept them, the students had to take buses to all-black schools in Knoxville.
Back cover: Young participants in the historic March on Washington in August 1963 join together to fight for civil rights.
Page one: Ruby Bridges was the first black student to attend William Franz Elementary School in New Orleans, Louisiana, in 1960. Nearly all of the white students withdrew from the school.
Page two: During a march for civil rights in Alabama, a young man carries the American flag.
Opposite page: John Lewis, second from left, leads a peaceful demonstration outside a swimming pool for whites only in Cairo, Illinois, in 1962.

Carolrhoda Books, Inc.
A division of Lerner Publishing Group
241 First Avenue North
Minneapolis, Minnesota 55401 U.S.A.

Website address: www.lernerbooks.com

LIBRARY OF CONGRESS CATALOGING-IN-PUBLICATION DATA

Welch, Catherine A.
  Children of the civil rights era / Catherine A. Welch
    p.   cm. — (Picture the American past)
  Includes bibliographical references and index.
  Summary: Recounts the courageous involvement of many young people who marched, protested, were arrested, and risked their lives to end racial discrimination in the South during the 1950s and 1960s.
  ISBN 1-57505-481-7 (alk. paper) lib. bdg.
  1. Afro-American children—Civil rights—History—20th century—Juvenile literature. 2. Children—Southern States—Political activity—Juvenile literature. 3. Afro-Americans—Civil rights—History—20th century—Juvenile literature. 4. Civil rights movements—Southern States—History—20th century—Juvenile literature. 5. Southern States—Race relations—Juvenile literature. [1. Civil rights—History. 2. Afro-Americans—Civil rights—History—20th century. 3. Civil rights movements—History—20th century. 4. Southern States—Race relations.] I. Title. II. Series.
E185.61.W42 2001
323.1'196073076'09045—dc21   00-008486

Manufactured in the United States of America
1 2 3 4 5 6 – JR – 06 05 04 03 02 01

CONTENTS

Above: In 1942, when this picture was taken, stores generally sold only white dolls, even though not all American children were white.
Opposite page: During the civil rights era, black children and adults marched and protested to gain equal rights with whites. While marching together, they chanted phrases such as "I am somebody" and "Freedom now."

THE BEGINNING

Tell me who's coming all dressed in white.
God's gonna trouble the water.
Well it looks like children fighting for their rights.
God's gonna trouble the water.
—from the spiritual "Wade in the Water"

Oh you better not call anybody black! That was a fighting word . . ." remembers Judy Tarver. Judy grew up in the 1950s. Back then, laws and attitudes made the United States a difficult place to grow up African American. Many African American children felt their skin was too dark, their hair too kinky. They thought white dolls looked nicer than black dolls.

But in the 1950s black Americans started a struggle for change. In those years, they started the civil rights movement.

Before the civil rights movement, black Americans in some parts of the United States could not send their laundry to the same cleaners as whites.

The civil rights movement was a struggle to change unfair laws. In the south, white people had passed laws and made rules. Some thought blacks were less than human. They wanted to keep blacks away from whites.

Blacks couldn't be buried next to whites in cemeteries. They couldn't check out books from libraries. In stores without restrooms for blacks, little children wet their pants and cried. Mothers stood by helpless. They felt like crying, too.

The civil rights movement was also a struggle to stop violence. In August 1955, Emmett Till—a fourteen-year-old boy from Chicago—was murdered in Mississippi. He was visiting relatives and didn't know the rules about not talking to whites.

At a country store, friends dared him to speak to a white woman. Emmett did and was killed for that.

Emmett Till was only fourteen when he was murdered after speaking to a white woman in Mississippi.

John Lewis was shocked when he heard of the killing. He was fifteen and black. *"That* could have been me . . . " he said.

Black children in the south worried. But they were also angry that they could not do simple things.

In the south, there were separate water fountains, schools, and waiting rooms for blacks and whites. This practice was called segregation.

On buses, blacks could not sit next to whites or in front of whites. If buses were crowded, blacks had to stand so whites could sit. Black people often had to give up their seats. After a hard day's work and a crowded bus ride, black mothers and fathers came home angry.

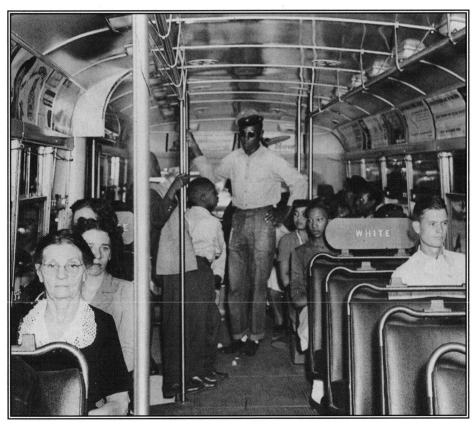

Birmingham, Alabama. Signs in this bus show the end of the section for white riders. Blacks paid the same fare but often stood while whites sat.

For some, anger turned to courage. On March 2, 1955, fifteen-year-old Claudette Colvin was riding a bus in Montgomery, Alabama. More and more white people got on. Claudette refused to give up her seat. In December, Rosa Parks did the same thing.

After both were arrested, blacks in Montgomery organized a protest. On December 5, they stopped riding the buses.

Montgomery, Alabama. Rosa Parks, a seamstress, was arrested by police for refusing to give up her bus seat to white riders. After the arrest, black organizers in Montgomery passed out thousands of leaflets urging blacks to stay off city buses.

Montgomery, Alabama. During the long months of the bus boycott, blacks organized car pools, walked, or hitched rides around town.

Black children walked to school. They laughed when near-empty buses rumbled by. "You wanted your buses, now you got 'em!"

Soon the bus company lost money, and whites grew angry. Some white teens drove past walking blacks, and threw rotten eggs, potatoes, and apples.

For almost thirteen months, blacks walked in rain, heat, and freezing temperatures. They stayed off buses until the bus company agreed to treat them with respect. Then they returned with a new feeling of power. Together they had changed one rule. Could other rules be changed?

Montgomery, Alabama. Rosa Parks was one of the first blacks to ride the buses after the bus company agreed to end separate seating.

Topeka, Kansas. Linda Brown (left), shown here with her sister, crossed railroad tracks to go to her all-black school. Her father fought in the courts to allow her to attend a white school closer to home. That case, Brown v. Board of Education of Topeka, made Linda a hero of the civil rights era.

White schools had newer books, more teachers, and better buildings than those for black children. Linda Brown had to cross dangerous railroad tracks to get to her black school in Topeka, Kansas. A white school was closer to her home. In 1954, the United States Supreme Court had said that black children *must* be allowed into white schools. But in the south, whites would not let blacks into their schools.

In 1957, nine black teenagers met with black leaders. They planned to enter a white school, Central High in Little Rock, Arkansas. At first, they were stopped by angry crowds. But President Eisenhower sent troops. They got the black teens safely into the school.

Melba Pattillo was one of the Little Rock Nine. She felt proud walking into the school. "Yes," she said to herself, "there is a reason I salute the flag, and it's going to be okay."

Little Rock, Arkansas. Eight of the first blacks to attend Central High School arrived together on the first day. But Elizabeth Eckford arrived on her own and had to face a crowd of screaming whites.

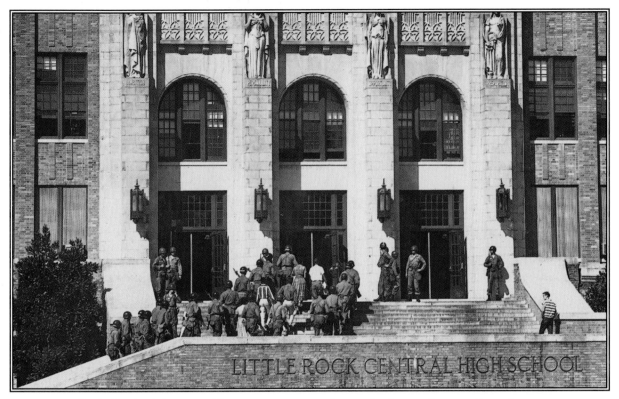

Little Rock, Arkansas. There were over two thousand white students at Central High. Though troops were present to keep the peace, the black students were not always safe.

In school, some white students were kind, but others were not. The black students were tripped and pushed on the stairs. One day, Jefferson Thomas was almost shoved into hot steam pipes. Another day, he was struck behind the ear.

Jeff's mother didn't want him to go to school the next day. But Jeff said, "No, if I stay out today, it'll be worse tomorrow."

Another day in school, firecrackers exploded around Gloria Ray. "I was so frightened I couldn't move," she said. "I was sure they were shooting at me."

Little Rock, Arkansas. The Little Rock Nine became close friends during their first year at Central High. They shared a dream that all black children might get a better education.

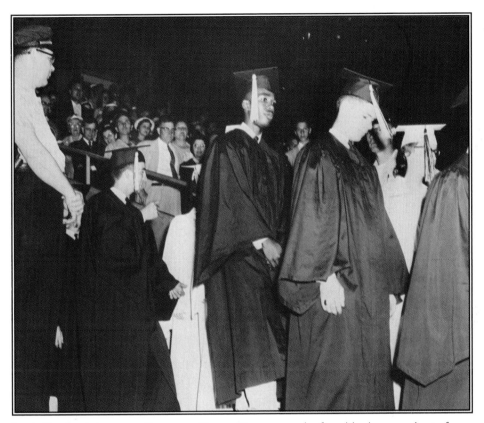

Little Rock, Arkansas. In 1958, Ernest Green was the first black to graduate from Central High. The largely white audience did not clap for him.

After Little Rock, it was easier for black children to go to a better school. But there were still many places where they could not go.

Throughout the south, blacks could buy things at dime stores, but they couldn't eat at the stores' lunch counters. Black college students decided it was time to change that rule.

Above: Black students who took part in sit-ins at dime store lunch counters didn't expect to be served food—at first. By filling seats that white, paying customers would otherwise fill, they hoped to persuade the counters' owners to serve all customers.

Opposite page: Many black students were arrested for sitting at lunch counters in Nashville, Tennessee, and other southern cities.

Lunch Counter Sit-Ins

We've met jail and violence too,
But God's love has seen us through,
Keep your eyes on the prize, hold on, hold on . . .
—from a civil rights song

In 1960, black college students in Nashville, Tennessee, and Greensboro, North Carolina, planned to sit at dime store lunch counters. They dressed neatly and brought books to study. They were prepared to sit for hours.

At the first Nashville sit-in, the white waitresses were nervous. They kept dropping dishes. Student Diane Nash remembers, "We were sitting there trying not to laugh . . . at the same time we were scared to death."

Angry whites attacked the sit-in students, but blacks did not fight back.

Anne Moody remembers a mob of white students coming into one store. They slapped, kicked, and threw blacks off the stools. A man slammed Anne against a counter.

"The mob started smearing us with ketchup, mustard, sugar, pies . . . " said Anne. The students prayed but did not fight back.

Before lunch counter sit-ins, students had gone to workshops. There they were trained to be nonviolent. Some pretended to be whites. They spit on the other black students. Angry students practiced not striking back.

"Finally, we sang. Then we prayed. Then we went home to sleep, if we could," said John Lewis.

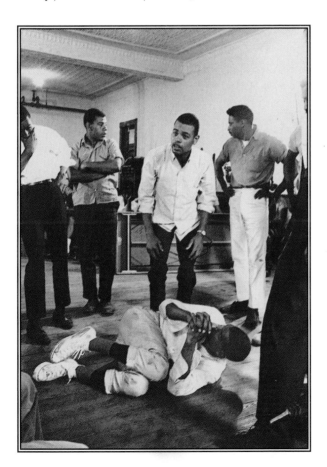

At nonviolence workshops before the sit-ins, students pretending to be white screamed the word nigger. The other students practiced remaining calm in the face of hate.

Nashville, Tennessee. Students such as John Lewis, wearing the light suit, were proud to be arrested during the sit-ins. They hoped to bring about change.

At sit-ins, white attackers were not arrested. Black students were. Police crowded them into trucks and took them to jail.

Parents were afraid for their children. Some parents were shocked and ashamed. They wanted their children out of the civil rights movement. But the students did not stop.

On April 19, 1960, someone destroyed the home of a lawyer who helped the sit-in students. That day, over two thousand angry students and adults marched to city hall. There, the mayor finally agreed that it was wrong not to serve blacks at lunch counters. Three weeks later, local lunch counters began serving blacks.

Nashville, Tennessee. From the bombed out home of their lawyer, the students marched to city hall, where they finally convinced the mayor that blacks should be served at all the city's lunch counters.

Above: People in Birmingham, Alabama, pray during a protest in 1963.
Opposite page: Children often went to church meetings where leaders organized
marches and protests. Leaders told them that if they did not stand up against
segregation, then they were responsible for it.

Marching toward Freedom

Black and white together, we shall not be moved . . .
We'll stand and fight together, we shall not be moved . . .
—from a civil rights song

Working together, black people brought change. But changing the rules in some places was very hard. In Birmingham, Alabama, blacks were often beaten, and their homes were bombed.

Many black adults were afraid to march and protest. They might lose their jobs and houses. So black leaders trained high school students, who had no jobs to lose.

In 1963, thousands of young people marched in Birmingham. They chanted, "We want freedom." Officer Bull Connor was in charge of keeping the public safe. But he attacked the marchers with high-powered water hoses. Children were knocked down by the strong blasts. Some were bitten by police dogs.

"Some people would . . . throw rocks and cans. . . ," Patricia Harris said. "I was afraid of getting hurt . . ."

Birmingham, Alabama. During marches in the spring of 1963, young people were attacked by fire hoses and police dogs.

Birmingham, Alabama. Danella Bryant was one of many young people who took part in protests. She paused for a moment to pray one day in May 1963.

Children were jailed. Nine-year-old Audrey Faye Hendricks was in jail for seven days. Parents cried and prayed.

Television news reports and newspapers around the world showed the children being attacked. People were shocked.

President Kennedy feared riots would break out across the country. In June, he spoke on television. He wanted to pass the Civil Rights Act to give blacks equal rights with whites.

The president's speech gave many people hope. But that very night, a hate-filled man shot the black leader Medgar Evers. His three children heard the gunfire that killed him outside their house in Jackson, Mississippi.

Blacks in the north also demonstrated for civil rights. They showed their support for the struggles of southern blacks and for the Civil Rights Act.

While Medgar Evers's children grieved, black leaders planned a march on Washington, D.C. In August 1963, people from north and south traveled to Washington. They were Catholics, Protestants, and Jews. Most were adults. Some were children. The crowd was angry but peaceful and hopeful.

Washington, D.C. At the March on Washington in August 1963, young marchers joined in the singing.

Washington, D.C. A young woman holds her program of events at the March on Washington. In the afternoon, Dr. Martin Luther King Jr. made his famous "I Have a Dream" speech.

That day, Dr. Martin Luther King Jr. spoke. With a strong, deep voice, he promised that blacks would keep fighting for their rights. He raised the hope that black and white children might someday join hands and live together. He prayed that we would all be "free at last."

Birmingham, Alabama. In September 1963, an explosion ripped a hole in the basement of the mostly black Sixteenth Street Baptist Church, injuring about twenty people and killing four young girls.

For some, a bomb shattered that hope the next month. It was a Sunday morning. A white man hid dynamite in a church in Birmingham, Alabama.

Four young girls died. Addie Mae Collins, Carole Robertson, and Cynthia Wesley were fourteen. Denise McNair was eleven. They were killed while changing into their choir robes.

The church bombing did not stop young people from working for civil rights. In 1964, the Civil Rights Act was passed, but there was still much to be done.

That summer, college students from all over the country went to Mississippi. Most were whites. They worked to get blacks signed up to vote.

Mississippi. Along with getting blacks signed up to vote, college students from the north organized Freedom Schools for black children and adults in the summer of 1964. Students learned reading, math, and black history.

During that summer, white students lived with black families. Seeing this disgusted some white southerners. They did not want blacks to mix with whites. They did not want blacks to vote. To frighten the students, southern whites killed three young people. Andrew Goodman and Michael Schwerner were whites from New York City. James Chaney was a black from Mississippi.

At a memorial service for his brother James—killed during the civil rights era— Ben Chaney sits beside his mother.

Selma, Alabama. On Sunday, March 7, 1965, not long after this photo was taken, peaceful marchers were attacked by police on horseback.

The murders scared people. But black leaders went ahead with plans to demand full voting rights. In Alabama, leaders planned to march from Selma to Montgomery. But when the marchers reached the Edmund Pettus Bridge in Selma, troops on horseback charged into the crowd.

Eight-year-old Sheyann Webb was there. She remembers horses clomping on the pavement. She ran just as tear gas started to burn her nose and eyes. "You'd hear people scream," she said, "and hear the whips swishing and you'd hear them striking people."

The marchers did not get to Montgomery that day. But two weeks later, they marched again.

Alabama. A second march from Selma to Montgomery on March 21 was successful. The president ordered troops to protect the twenty-five thousand people who took part.

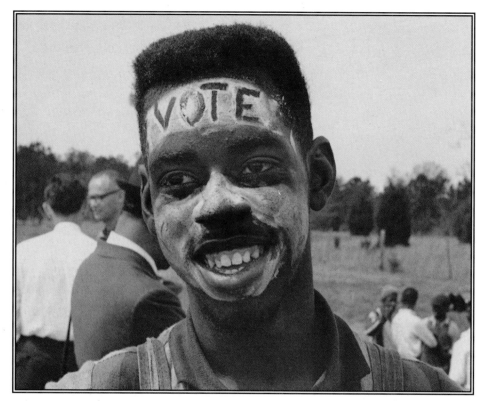

Many young people demonstrated in support of the Voting Rights Act of 1965. Before the act was passed, whites in the south often made blacks take tests to see if they were qualified to vote. The tests were so unfair that most blacks failed.

In 1965, Congress passed the Voting Rights Act. This law stated that no one could stop blacks from voting. It stated that blacks would be protected at voting places in all elections.

Children too young to vote had helped pass the Voting Rights Act. They had helped African Americans gain *real* power to make changes in the country.

The children of the civil rights era were heroes. They marched, protested, and were arrested. Some risked their lives.

Rachel West was nine when she marched. "It would have been easier to stay inside, sprawled on my belly watching the cartoons," she said. "I was scared . . . But the people would sing with us, and we'd help each other overcome the fear."

Alabama. The Civil Rights Monument, built in 1989, records the dates, events, and heroes—young and old—of the civil rights era.

Learning about Nonviolence

John Lewis was a college student and one of the young leaders of the civil rights movement. He protested against segregation and marched for civil rights. In 1960, he took part in the lunch counter sit-ins in Nashville, Tennessee. He was asked to write a list of "dos" and "don'ts" for other protesters to follow. Below is John Lewis's Nashville Code:

1. *Don't strike back or curse if abused.*
2. *Don't laugh out.*
3. *Don't hold conversations with floor workers.*
4. *Don't block entrances to the stores or aisles.*
5. *Show yourself courteous and friendly at all times.*
6. *Sit straight and always face the counter.*
7. *Remember love and nonviolence.*
8. *May God bless each of you.*

Which modern protesters seem to be following John Lewis's Nashville Code? Follow the steps below to see how people in your community and state are using nonviolent action to bring about change.

1. Read community newspapers and watch the news on television. Look for information about people in your area who are working to bring about change. Maybe some protesters want to keep land from being turned into a shopping mall. Maybe a group of workers is demanding better pay or safer conditions in their workplace. Try to find out about the work of more than one group. Take notes about what you learn.

2. Reread John Lewis's Nashville Code. Are the nonviolent methods Lewis described being used by the groups you studied? For example, have people staged a peaceful and courteous protest in support of their cause? Or did they block entrances to buildings, curse at or attack others, or damage property? Make a list of the methods you see at work.

3. Compare and contrast the methods used by the different groups you are studying. Which groups seemed to get what they wanted? Which used nonviolent methods? Which did not? How could these groups have done things differently?

4. Invite those who have used nonviolent methods to visit your school and talk about their work. If you can't arrange a visit, ask these people if you might interview them by phone or in person.

5. Learn more about nonviolent action by studying the following resources: *The Kid's Guide to Social Action* by Barbara Lewis (Minneapolis: Free Spirit, 1991) is a resource guide for young activists; *The Power of the People: Active Nonviolence in the United States,* edited by Robert Cooney and Helen Michalowski (Philadelphia: New Society Publishers, 1987) covers the history of peaceful protests in the United States and provides profiles of many important activists.

6. Gather your information and share what you've learned about nonviolence. You could make a bulletin-board display of your findings, write an article for the school newspaper, or create a page for your school's website.

NOTE TO TEACHERS AND ADULTS

For children, the civil rights era may seem like part of a far-off past. But there are many ways to make this era and its people come alive. Along with encouraging children to use nonviolent action to solve problems and bring about change, you can explore America's civil rights past in other ways. One way is to read more about the era. More books on the topic are listed on pages 45 and 46. Another way to explore the past is to train young readers to study historical photographs. Historical photographs hold many clues about how life was lived in earlier times.

Ask your children or students to look for the details and "read" all the information in each picture in this book. For example, under segregation, what kinds of activities were blacks forced to do apart from whites?

To encourage young readers to learn to read historical photographs, have them try these activities:

Writing Letters, Spreading the News

From the point of view, or perspective, of one of the children shown in this book, write a letter to a friend in the north or in another country telling about the civil rights struggles in your hometown. What do you hope to change? What methods will you and others use? Do you want your friend or relative to join you in the struggle? To learn more about young civil rights heroes, read some of the books listed on pages 45 and 46, including *Freedom's Children, Leon's Story,* and *Selma, Lord, Selma.* Study the photographs in this book to add details about daily life and civil rights struggles.

Looking at Protests

Study the photographs of people taking part in protests in this book. On a piece of paper in one column, under the heading "Civil Rights Era," write down all the different ways of protesting and bringing about change that you see. Next, ask a teacher, parent, or librarian to help you study a modern protest movement. Some examples are protests against raising animals for their fur, against or in support of cutting down trees in old-growth forests, and against the use of poorly paid sweatshop workers in making clothing. Study articles about and photographs of modern protests and protesters. Under the heading "In My Era," write down all the different ways of protesting or bringing about change that you see. What conclusions can you draw about how protests have changed since the 1950s and 1960s? How have protests stayed the same? How do you think protests will be different in another fifty years?

Gathering Memories

Many older Americans have vivid memories of civil rights struggles. Whether they directly took part in the movement or recall television news reports, their memories can tell you a great deal about what America was like in the 1950s and 1960s. Set aside time to interview older friends or your grandparents. Ask them what they remember about the civil rights era. How do they think life has changed in the years since? Can they think of ways in which protests and marches helped bring about changes? To learn more about interviewing people, read Casey King and Linda Barrett Osborne's book, *Oh Freedom! Kids Talk about the Civil Rights Movement with the People Who Made It Happen.*

RESOURCES ON THE CIVIL RIGHTS ERA

Coleman, Evelyn. *White Socks Only.* Morton Grove, IL: Albert Whitman & Company, 1996. In this picture book, a young black girl walks into town on a hot day to see if she can fry an egg on the sidewalk. When she drinks from a "Whites Only" drinking fountain, she creates a stir.

Curtis, Christopher Paul. *The Watsons Go to Birmingham—1963.* New York: Delacorte Press, 1995. In this novel for middle-grade readers, the eccentric, entertaining Watson family of Flint, Michigan, travels to Birmingham, Alabama, to see their relatives.

Darby, Jean. *Martin Luther King, Jr.* Minneapolis, MN: Lerner Publications Company, 1990. Darby tells the story of the great civil rights leader Dr. Martin Luther King, Jr., describing his philosophy of nonviolence and explaining key events in his struggle for racial equality.

King, Casey, and Linda Barrett Osborne. *Oh Freedom! Kids Talk about the Civil Rights Movement with the People Who Made It Happen.* New York: Alfred A. Knopf, 1997. Children interview activists and ordinary citizens, both black and white, about their experiences during the civil rights era.

Levine, Ellen. *Freedom's Children: Young Civil Rights Activists Tell Their Own Stories.* New York: G.P. Putnam's Sons, 1993. Levine focuses on the experiences of black children and teenagers, interviewed as adults, who worked for civil rights.

Lucas, Eileen. *Cracking the Wall: The Struggles of the Little Rock Nine.* Minneapolis, MN: Carolrhoda Books, Inc., 1997. In this book for beginning readers, Lucas recalls the struggles of the nine black teenagers, interviewed as adults, who attended all-white Central High School in Little Rock, Arkansas, in 1957.

Moore, Yvette. *Freedom Songs.* New York: Puffin Books, 1991. During a visit to relatives in North Carolina, fourteen-year-old Sheryl from Brooklyn encounters segregation and discrimination in this novel for middle-grade readers.

Tillage, Leon Walter. *Leon's Story.* New York: Farrar, Straus & Giroux, 1997. Leon Tillage remembers his youth in North Carolina during the 1940s and 1950s, when he went to an all-black school, hid from hate-filled whites, and took part in civil rights marches.

Webb, Sheyann, and Rachel West Nelson. *Selma, Lord, Selma: Girlhood Memories of the Civil-Rights Days.* Tuscaloosa, AL: The University of Alabama Press, 1980. Sheyann Webb was eight and Rachel West was nine when they became part of the civil rights movement in Selma, Alabama. They recall the demonstrations and the dangers they faced.

Website <http://seattletimes.nwsource.com/mlk/movement/PT/phototour.html> Take a photo tour of the civil rights movement on this website. Follow the link for "The Movement" and learn about Martin Luther King Jr.

NEW WORDS

boycott: a planned buyers' strike intended to make the seller change policy

civil rights: personal liberties to which citizens are entitled

Civil Rights Act of 1964: a law enabling blacks and other minorities to enjoy personal liberties—such as finding a job, voting, or staying in hotels or motels—without fear of discrimination

dime stores: department stores stocking inexpensive goods

Freedom Schools: informal study groups and schools for blacks taught by volunteers in Mississippi in the summer of 1964

segregation: the separation of one from another, generally isolating a minority group from the majority

sit-in: the act of demanding service in a segregated place by taking up seats

Voting Rights Act of 1965: a law giving blacks protection in voting places and enabling large numbers of southern blacks to vote for the first time

INDEX

TIME LINE

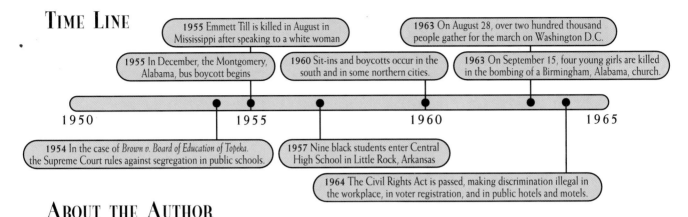

1955 Emmett Till is killed in August in Mississippi after speaking to a white woman

1963 On August 28, over two hundred thousand people gather for the march on Washington D.C.

1955 In December, the Montgomery, Alabama, bus boycott begins

1960 Sit-ins and boycotts occur in the south and in some northern cities.

1963 On September 15, four young girls are killed in the bombing of a Birmingham, Alabama, church.

1950   1955   1960   1965

1954 In the case of *Brown v. Board of Education of Topeka*. the Supreme Court rules against segregation in public schools.

1957 Nine black students enter Central High School in Little Rock, Arkansas

1964 The Civil Rights Act is passed, making discrimination illegal in the workplace, in voter registration, and in public hotels and motels.

ABOUT THE AUTHOR

Catherine A. Welch lives in Monroe, Connecticut, with her husband and two children. She is the author of several books for children published by Carolrhoda, including *Margaret Bourke-White: Racing with a Dream, Ida B. Wells-Barnett: Powerhouse with a Pen,* and *Children of the Relocation Camps.*

ACKNOWLEDGMENTS

The author thanks the following people, who helped in gathering material for this book: Ingrid Davis, Mary Ellen Delaney, and the staff of the Monroe, CT, Public Library. The publisher gratefully acknowledges the use of quotations from the following sources: Daisy Bates, *The Long Shadow of Little Rock: A Memoir.* Fayetteville, AR: The University of Arkansas Press, 1986 (Reprinted by permission of the University of Arkansas Press. Copyright 1986 by Daisy Bates); Guy and Candie Carawan, *Sing for Freedom.* Traditional lyrics adapted by Sam Block and Willie Peacock [SNCC]. Copyright 1963, 1990 by SingOut Corporation); David J. Garrow, editor, *The Montgomery Bus Boycott and the Women Who Started It: The Memoir of Jo Ann Gibson Robinson.* Knoxville, TN: University of Tennessee Press, 1987; Henry Hampton and Steve Fayer with Sarah Flynn, *Voices of Freedom: An Oral History of the Civil Rights Movement from the 1950s through the 1980s.* New York: Bantam Books, 1990; Mary King, *Freedom's Song: A Personal Story of the 1960s Civil Rights Movement.* New York: William Morrow and Co. Inc., 1987; Ellen Levine, *Freedom's Children: Young Civil Rights Activists Tell Their Own Stories.* New York: G. P. Putnam's Sons, 1993; John Lewis with Michael D'Orso, *Walking with the Wind: A Memoir of the Movement.* New York: Simon & Schuster, 1998; Danny Lyon, *Memories of the Southern Civil Rights Movement.* Chapel Hill, NC: University of North Carolina Press, 1992; Anne Moody, *Coming of Age in Mississippi.* New York: Dial, 1968; Sheyann Webb and Rachel West Nelson, *Selma, Lord, Selma: Girlhood Memories of the Civil-Rights Days.* Tuscaloosa, AL: The University of Alabama Press, 1980; Juan Williams, *Eyes on the Prize: America's Civil Rights Years, 1954-1965.* New York: Penguin Books, 1987. The photographs in this book are reproduced through the courtesy of: The Library of Congress, front cover [LC-USZ62-116819], pp. 6 [LC-USF34-013426-C], 26 [LC-USZ62-110972]; © Bettmann/Corbis, back cover, pp. 9, 10, 14, 16, 18, 19, 20, 22, 25, 28, 30; Corbis/Bettman-UPI, pp. 1, 29, 38; © James H. Karales, pp. 2, 37; Magnum Photos Inc. © 1962 Danny Lyon, pp. 5, 23; © Flip Schulke/Corbis, pp. 7, 27, 36; Schomburg Center for Research in Black Culture, p. 8; Courtesy of Birmingham Public Library, pp. 11 [49.59], 33 [85.1.22]; AP/Wide World Photos, pp. 12, 13; Carl Iwasaki/Life Magazine © TIME Inc., p. 15; Arkansas Democrat-Gazette, p. 17; The Tennessean, pp. 21, 24; National Archives, pp. 31 [NWDNS-306-SSM-4C(19)3], 32 [NWDNS-306-SSM-4C(53)28]; State Historical Society of Wisconsin, p. 34 [WHi (X3)45642]; ©Kenneth Thompson/General Board of Global Ministries, 35; Alabama Bureau of Tourism & Travel, p. 39.